Geek out!

A MODERN NERD'S GUIDE TO

COMIC BOOKS

BY NICOLE HORNING

Gareth Stevens
PUBLISHING

Please visit our website, www.garethstevens.com. For a free color catalog of all our high-quality books, call toll free 1-800-542-2595 or fax 1-877-542-2596.

Cataloging-in-Publication Data

Names: Horning, Nicole.
Title: A modern nerd's guide to comic books / Nicole Horning.
Description: New York : Gareth Stevens Publishing, 2020. | Series: Geek out! | Includes glossary and index.
Identifiers: ISBN 9781538240069 (pbk.) | ISBN 9781538240090 (library bound) | ISBN 9781538240076 (6 pack)
Subjects: LCSH: Comic books, strips, etc.–United States–Juvenile literature. | Comic books, strips, etc.–United States–History and criticism–Juvenile literature.
Classification: LCC PN6725.H67 2020 | DDC 741.5′973–dc23

First Edition

Published in 2020 by
Gareth Stevens Publishing
111 East 14th Street, Suite 349
New York, NY 10003

Copyright © 2020 Gareth Stevens Publishing

Designer: Sarah Liddell
Editor: Abby Badach Doyle

Photo credits: Cover, p. 1 StockPhotosArt/Shutterstock.com; texture used throughout StrelaStudio/Shutterstock.com; p. 5 ROBYN BECK/Contributor/AFP/Getty Images; p. 6 Christian Mueller/Shutterstock.com; p. 7 photo courtesy of Library of Congress; p. 9 Hulton Archive/Handout/Moviepix/Getty Images; p. 11 AFP Contributor/Contributor/AFP/Getty Images; p. 12 Studio Matitanera/Shutterstock.com; p. 13 Roberto Serra - Iguana Press/Contributor/Getty Images Entertainment/Getty Images; p. 15 Keylimepie222/Wikimedia Commons; p. 16 AFP/Stringer/AFP/Getty Images; p. 17 PAU BARRENA/Stringer/AFP/Getty Images; p. 18 Boston Globe/Contributor/Boston Globe/Getty Images; p. 19 Jack Taylor/Stringer/Getty Images News/Getty Images; p. 21 Koichi Kamoshida/Staff/Getty Images Entertainment/Getty Images; p. 25 Radu Bercan/Shutterstock.com; p. 26 RHONA WISE/Stringer/AFP/Getty Images; p. 27 Barbara Davidson/Contributor/Los Angeles Times/Getty Images; p. 29 Alberto E. Rodriguez/Staff/Getty Images Entertainment/Getty Images.

Printed in the United States of America

CPSIA compliance information: Batch #CS19GS: For further information contact Gareth Stevens, New York, New York at 1-800-542-2595.

CONTENTS

Words in the glossary appear in **bold** type the first time they are used in the text.

A COMIC FOR EVERYONE

Spider-Man gets bitten by a spider and helps people with the powers he gains. Captain America receives the Super-Soldier **serum** to boost his strength and intelligence. Action-packed movies featuring these characters are fun and **fascinating** . . . but maybe you want to know more. Where did these characters come from? What else have they done?

Comic books are filled with even more exciting stories! Characters like Captain America, Spider-Man, Wonder Woman, Batman, and more all started in popular comic books. Not all comic books are about superheroes. There are many comic books to fit your interests, like science fiction, history, or animals.

THE GEEK COMMUNITY

A "nerd" or a "geek" is a person who deeply **appreciates** something. It could be a book or movie, or it could be a certain superhero or comic universe. Being a geek is about sharing interests with a group of people and being a part of that community. Embrace your inner geek!

Spider-Man is one of the most famous superheroes. He first appeared in comic books in the 1960s.

COMICS: A HISTORY

In 1842, the cartoon *The Adventures of Obadiah Oldbuck* appeared in a US newspaper. It wasn't exactly like today's comics, but it was similar. It didn't catch on like other comics would much later, but it made other illustrators and authors want to give this form of storytelling a try.

In the 1890s, comic strips began appearing in newspapers. At that time, authors and illustrators **introduced** two important elements of comics that are still used today. The first one was speech bubbles to show what the characters were saying. The second was using panels to tell stories one picture at a time.

Charles Schulz created the comic strip *Peanuts* using the classic panel format.

PEANUTS

One of the most famous newspaper comic strips is *Peanuts*, created by Charles Schulz. It first appeared in newspapers in 1950. The final new *Peanuts* comic was published in 2000. Some of the most loved characters in comics and movies, such as Charlie Brown and Snoopy, came from this comic strip.

The years 1938 through 1950 are known as the Golden Age of comics. Many famous comic characters were created during this time. In 1938, Superman first appeared in *Action Comics No. 1*. It was published by Detective Comics, Inc., which would later be known as DC Comics. Shortly after, DC added more superheroes, including Batman in 1939 and Wonder Woman in 1941.

During World War II, comic books became a popular form of entertainment. In March 1941, Marvel released the first *Captain America* comic book. In its pages, the hero was shown fighting the United States' real-life enemies from the war!

SUPERMAN

Superman is one of the best-known comic book heroes. He was created by writer Jerry Siegel and illustrator Joe Shuster, who grew up together in Cleveland, Ohio. They sold their creation to DC Comics. Superman became so popular with readers that he later got his own comic.

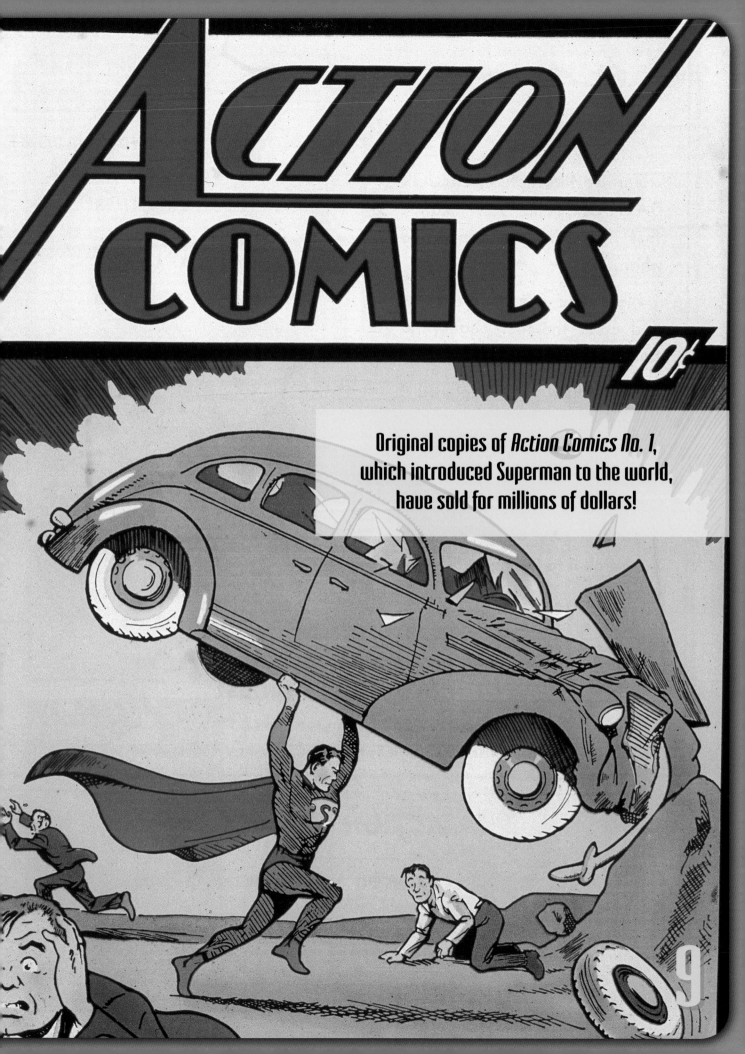

Original copies of *Action Comics No. 1*, which introduced Superman to the world, have sold for millions of dollars!

9

COMIC COMPANIES

When you're starting to read comics, you will come across many comic book companies. Each one has its own cast of characters to write about. While there are many companies, there are two main ones that are often called "the big two."

The "big two" companies are DC Comics and Marvel. Some fans prefer one company over the other because they prefer a certain type of superhero. There are even fans who **debate** over which company is better! Other fans enjoy the work of both companies and have favorite superheroes from each one.

DC EXTENDED UNIVERSE

The DC Extended Universe (DCEU) **refers** to a series of superhero movies based on DC Comics. The superheroes whose stories are told in the DCEU include Batman, Wonder Woman, Superman, Aquaman, and more. These characters each have their own movies, but they also appear in the *Justice League* together.

The superhero movie *Justice League* premiered in 2017. The cast includes (from left to right) Ezra Miller, Jason Momoa, Gal Gadot, Ben Affleck, Ray Fisher, and Henry Cavill.

Marvel creates its characters as regular people with superpowers. The stories take place in real cities. This made readers feel like Captain America or Spider-Man could actually appear where they lived! Characters in Marvel comics have longer backstories, or history. Characters can appear in each other's comics, giving the feel of a larger story.

Characters in the DC Comics universe exist in imaginary places, like Gotham City. DC Comics focuses on an individual character's story instead of how they fit into the larger universe the company has created. This means the character doesn't have as much of a background that is necessary to know to start reading.

Jack Kirby had a bold imagination and found ways to illustrate comics that no artist had done before.

JACK KIRBY

JACK KIRBY

Jack Kirby was a writer, artist, and editor at the comic company Marvel. He created some of its most famous characters. Some of the creations he worked on that are still popular today are Captain America, Thor, the Avengers, the X-Men, and the Fantastic Four.

WHERE TO GET COMICS

Comic books have existed for so long that it might feel **overwhelming** to start reading them now. Some characters, such as Captain America and Batman, have been around for more than 80 years! Luckily, there are lots of places to get comics and meet kids who are interested in comics, too.

You can ask an adult to take you to your local comic book store, or you can go to your local library to borrow comics. Some companies, such as Marvel, even have digital comics that you can read online with an adult's permission. Comic books can also be purchased at comic **conventions**.

COMIC RATING SYSTEMS

Not all comic books are written for kids. Some books have age **restrictions** and are created for teenagers or adults. These comic books may have a small "T", "T+", or other sticker that lets you know these comics are only for older readers.

WHERE TO GET COMIC BOOKS

- BOOKSTORE
- LIBRARY
- COMIC BOOK SHOP
- ONLINE (DIGITAL COMICS)
- COMIC CONVENTIONS

Ready to buy or borrow your first comic book? You have a lot of choices! Which place do you want to visit first?

READING COMIC BOOKS

Now that you know where to find comics, it's time to dive in and read! Where should you start? Maybe there is a character you like in a Marvel or DC movie. Don't worry about not having new stories to read about those characters. The movies usually cover only a very small piece of it. Sometimes, a story is changed for the movie version.

Superhero comics are the most popular, but there are many other types of comic books to choose from. There are comic books based on Disney movies, TV shows such as *Scooby Doo*, and video games such as *Sonic the Hedgehog*.

There are many types of comic books to choose from. What story or superhero sounds the most interesting to you?

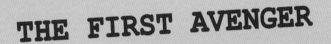

THE FIRST AVENGER

Captain America is one of the longest-running comic book series, but it was **canceled** twice before it took off. The series follows Steve Rogers, who gets the Super-Soldier serum and becomes Captain America. Other characters also have storylines where they become Captain America, but Steve Rogers always returns to fight **villains** with his famous shield.

TAKE YOUR TIME!

You don't have to know everything about a character or comic company to be a fan! It's important to have fun with what you're reading and explore the story in the way you want to. Take your time learning about the character and enjoy the process.

Comic books aren't written by the same author throughout the whole series. Instead, there are "runs." This means a certain writer will take over the series for a certain amount of time, generally for a couple of years. Often the best point to start with a comic book series is at the beginning of the most recent run by an author.

Once you decide what author run to read, you may need to know some backstories of the characters. Many characters have **encyclopedias** created about them with fun facts and details. Some comic companies have character biographies, or life stories, on their websites.

Batman, also called "The Caped Crusader" or "The Dark Knight," is a good example of a comic character with a lot of backstory.

ONE WORLD, MANY STORIES

When there are many authors writing different runs of comic book characters, sometimes an author changes something in a storyline that a previous author did. It can be a small change, or something that reimagines the story in a whole different way. The authors of the story want the change to be good for the character or storyline . . . but sometimes, fans don't agree.

For example, the storyline may need to be updated for new readers or a character's background may need to change for the new story. These edits can be made in the comics themselves, or the movie renditions of the story.

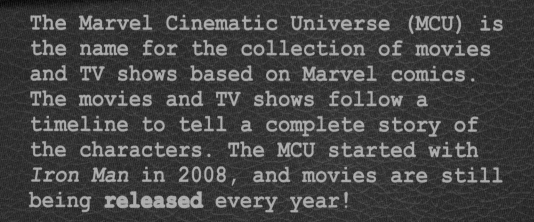

MARVEL CINEMATIC UNIVERSE

The Marvel Cinematic Universe (MCU) is the name for the collection of movies and TV shows based on Marvel comics. The movies and TV shows follow a timeline to tell a complete story of the characters. The MCU started with *Iron Man* in 2008, and movies are still being **released** every year!

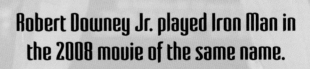

Robert Downey Jr. played Iron Man in the 2008 movie of the same name.

21

HOW TO STORE COMICS

Once you start reading and collecting comic books, caring for them is important so they can stay in good condition and you can read them again later. First, single-issue comics should be stored in a comic book sleeve with a comic book board. These keep the comic flat and stop the pages from bending and getting ripped.

Once you have your single-issue comic in a bag with a board, you have to decide how you want to store your comics. Comics can be stored standing upright in a cardboard or plastic box, or you can display them in a bookcase.

VALUE OF COMIC ISSUES

Single-issue comics can sometimes be worth a lot of money if they are in good condition. Some rare comics have sold for millions of dollars! Comic books that are worth the most are often from the 1930s to the 1970s. A comic book is graded based on how it looks and feels.

FORMATS OF COMICS

SINGLE ISSUE: THESE COMICS LOOK LIKE THIN MAGAZINES AND ARE OFTEN NUMBERED.

DIGITAL COMICS: THESE COMICS CAN BE READ ON A COMPUTER, SMARTPHONE, OR TABLET.

TRADE PAPERBACK: THE MOST COMMON TYPE OF COLLECTION, THESE FEATURE BETWEEN FIVE AND EIGHT SINGLE ISSUES IN ONE BOOK.

HARDCOVER: HARDCOVERS CAN SOMETIMES COLLECT ABOUT 12 SINGLE ISSUES, BUT OFTEN IT IS THE SAME AMOUNT OF ISSUES AS THE TRADE PAPERBACK.

OMNIBUS: OMNIBUSES ARE VERY LARGE COLLECTIONS, OFTEN WITH 25 OR MORE SINGLE ISSUES. THEY CAN FEATURE AN AUTHOR'S RUN OR THE ENTIRE SERIES.

ORIGINAL GRAPHIC NOVEL: THIS REFERS TO A COMIC BOOK THAT DIDN'T HAVE SINGLE ISSUES RELEASED BEFORE BEING PUBLISHED.

Comic books come in many forms. These are some of the most common ways comic books are sold.

COMIC BOOK STORES

Comic book stores are not just a place to buy comics. They are also a great place to talk with other fans! The people who work at the store are often happy to give suggestions of other comics to read. They may even be able to answer questions you have about a comic or tell you where you could look for the answer.

Some stores also sell things related to comics, such as T-shirts and collectible items. Sometimes, comic book stores have fun special events. It could be a costume contest around Halloween or a themed event for a certain comic book character!

FREE COMIC BOOK DAY

Free Comic Book Day happens the first Saturday in May at comic book stores. Each year, publishers put out free comic books to give away at comic book stores. The stores celebrate with fun events and costumes. If you aren't sure what to read, this annual event is a great place to start!

Each comic book store is set up differently. Some comic book stores also have mugs, T-shirts, toys, and games.

COMIC CONVENTIONS

Comic conventions, or comic cons, are a fun place to be around other comic book fans. At a convention, you can also meet and talk with your favorite comic book authors, artists, and even the actors who have played your favorite characters in movies!

Comic cons have areas with toys or other collectible items. Still, one of the most popular things at conventions are the comic books! You can see old single issues of comic books and buy books with multiple single issues collected together. Many people even dress up as their favorite comic character. Fans call that costume play, or "cosplay" for short.

Stan Lee was the leader of Marvel Comics for many years. Some fans were able to meet him at comic conventions. He died in 2018.

STAN LEE

Stan Lee was a very important person to comic book fans. His career began in 1939. His first writing project was creating a story in *Captain America* #3. In the 1960s, he was sometimes the only writer working on comics at Marvel and co-created popular characters including Iron Man, Thor, the X-Men, and the Avengers.

27

THE FUTURE OF COMIC BOOKS

Today, people have many comics to choose from. There are thousands of comic characters to read about, from classic stories to new ones. In early comics, superheroes were almost always men. In many new comics, women and girls are taking the lead!

The Unstoppable Wasp combines science, technology, and superheroes in a fun series that also has cameos from other female superheroes, such as Ms. Marvel. Marvel also publishes *The Unbeatable Squirrel Girl*, which is a fun comic book about a girl with squirrel-like superpowers. With these characters and many others, comic books are becoming more diverse, which means there is something for everyone!

MOON GIRL

Lunella Lafayette, another Marvel hero, is a 9-year-old genius who has an unusual friend ... a dinosaur! She is linked with the dinosaur and switches brains with it. Once she is linked with the dinosaur, she turns into Moon Girl and is able to protect the world with her superpowers!

Marvel's 2019 movie, *Captain Marvel*, features a female lead for the first time in the company's movies! Brie Larson stars as Captain Marvel, which is based on the comic book of the same name.

BRIE LARSON

GLOSSARY

appreciate: to understand the worth or importance of something

cancel: to decide that something will not happen

convention: a large meeting of people who come to a place to talk about their shared interests

debate: to argue a side

encyclopedia: a book that contains information about many subjects or a lot of information about a particular subject

fascinating: very interesting or appealing

introduce: to cause something to be used for the first time

overwhelming: when something is so confusing or difficult that you feel unable to do it

refer: to have a connection to something

release: to make something ready for use or sale

restriction: a law or rule that limits or controls something

serum: a powerful liquid used in science or medicine

villain: a person or character who does bad things

FOR MORE INFORMATION

BOOKS

Carbaugh, Samuel. *Comics: Investigate the History and Technology of American Cartooning.* White River Junction, VT: Nomad Press, 2014.

Forbeck, Matt. *Marvel Encyclopedia.* New York, NY: DK, 2014.

Manning, Matthew K., and Alex Irvine. *The DC Comics Encyclopedia: The Definitive Guide to the Characters of the DC Universe.* New York, NY: DK, 2014.

WEBSITES

DC
www.dccomics.com
DC Comics' website has information on all things DC, including games, collectibles, videos, and sneak peeks of upcoming comics.

Free Comic Book Day
www.freecomicbookday.com
This website has comic news, and you can search on the website to see what comic stores are participating in Free Comic Day.

Marvel
www.marvel.com
This website has character information and news on comic books and Marvel movies.

INDEX